STIRLING · ALLOA

BRIDGE OF ALLAN · DUNBLANE

KT-871-380

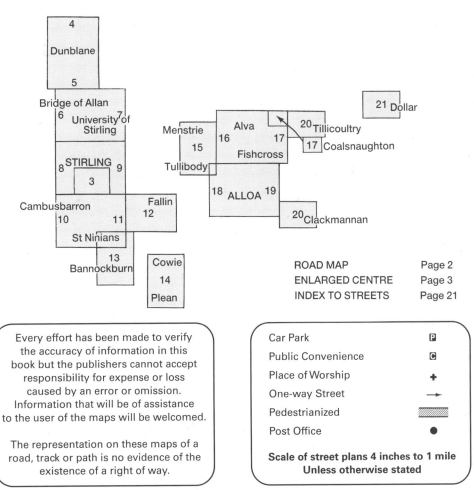

ROAD MAP — Page 2
ENLARGED CENTRE — Page 3
INDEX TO STREETS — Page 21

Every effort has been made to verify the accuracy of information in this book but the publishers cannot accept responsibility for expense or loss caused by an error or omission. Information that will be of assistance to the user of the maps will be welcomed.

The representation on these maps of a road, track or path is no evidence of the existence of a right of way.

Car Park	ℙ
Public Convenience	ⓒ
Place of Worship	+
One-way Street	→
Pedestrianized	▨
Post Office	●

Scale of street plans 4 inches to 1 mile
Unless otherwise stated

Street plans prepared and published by ESTATE PUBLICATIONS, Bridewell House, TENTERDEN, KENT.
The Publishers acknowledge the co-operation of the local authorities of towns represented in this atlas.

Ordnance Survey® This product includes mapping data licensed from Ordnance Survey® with the permission of the Controller of Her Majesty's Stationery Office.

Scale 2½ miles to 1 inch

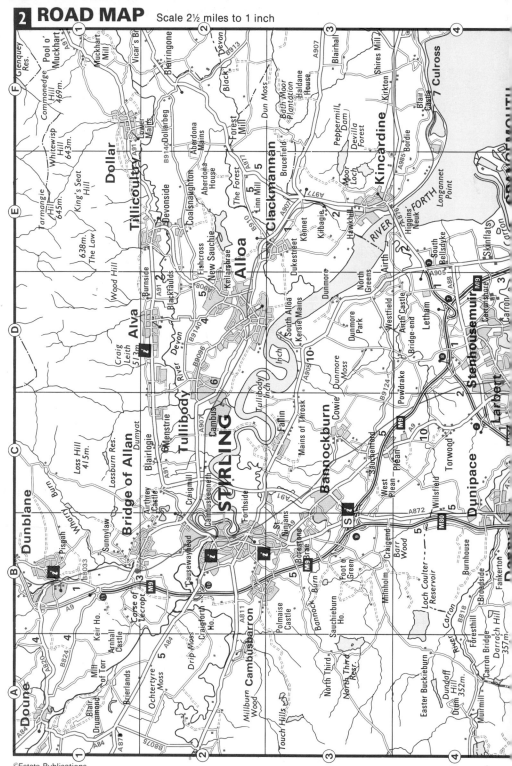

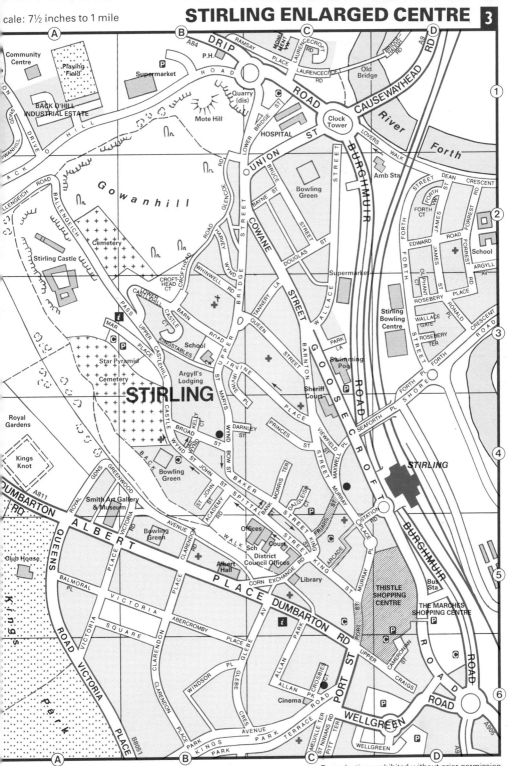

Scale: 7½ inches to 1 mile

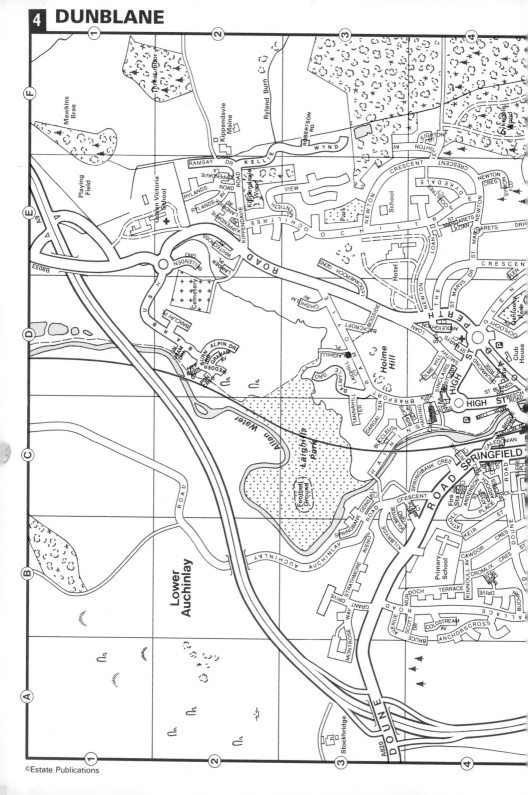

4 DUNBLANE

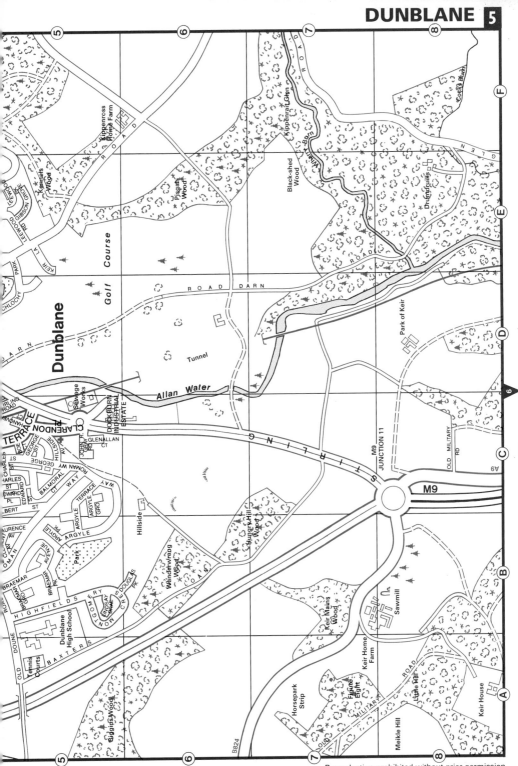

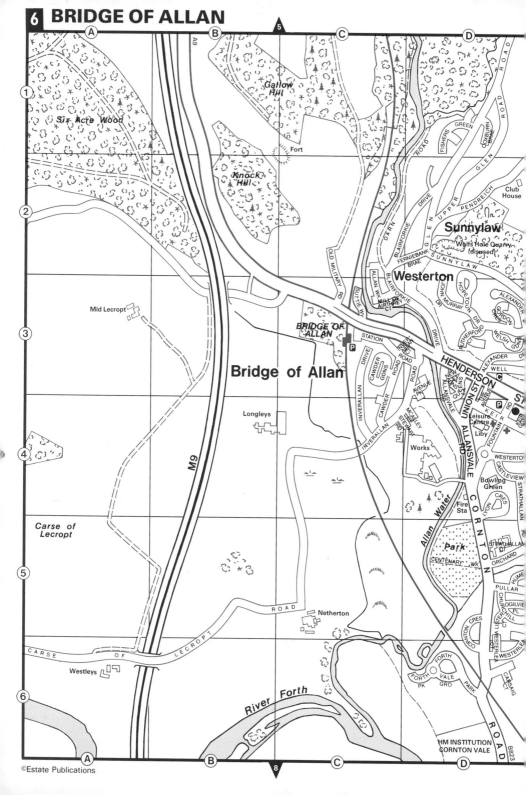

6 BRIDGE OF ALLAN

©Estate Publications

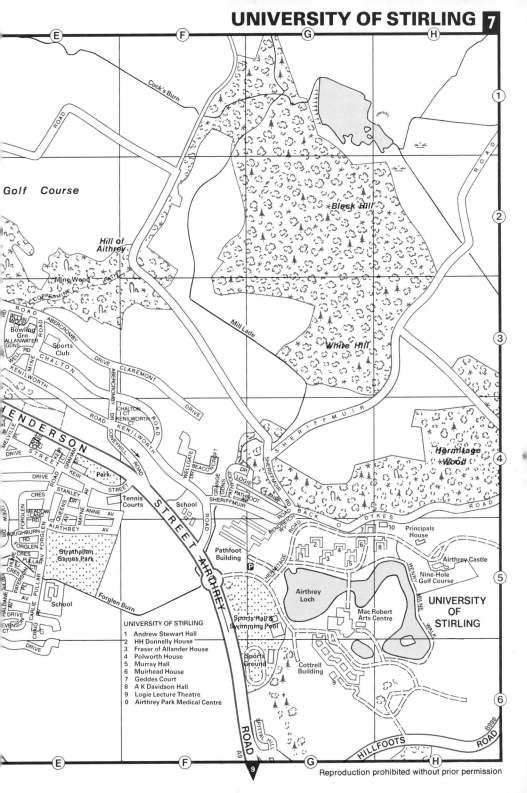

UNIVERSITY OF STIRLING

1 Andrew Stewart Hall
2 HH Donnelly House
3 Fraser of Allander House
4 Polworth House
5 Murray Hall
6 Muirhead House
7 Geddes Court
8 A K Davidson Hall
9 Logie Lecture Theatre
0 Airthrey Park Medical Centre

8 STIRLING

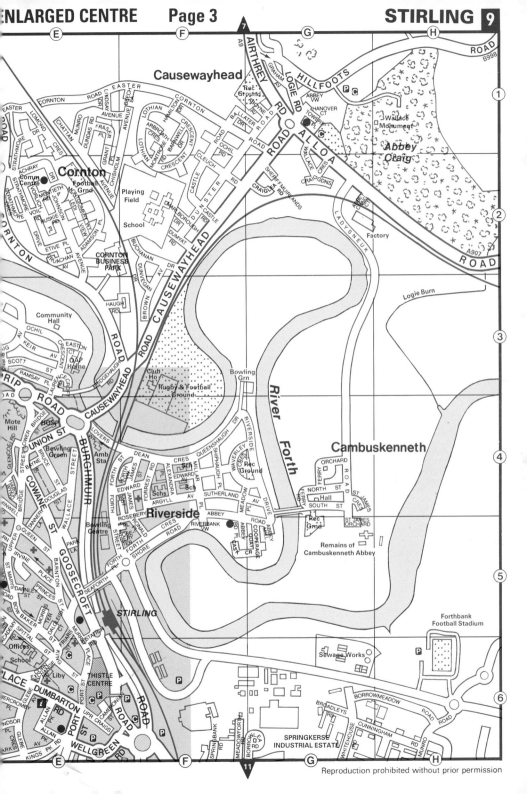

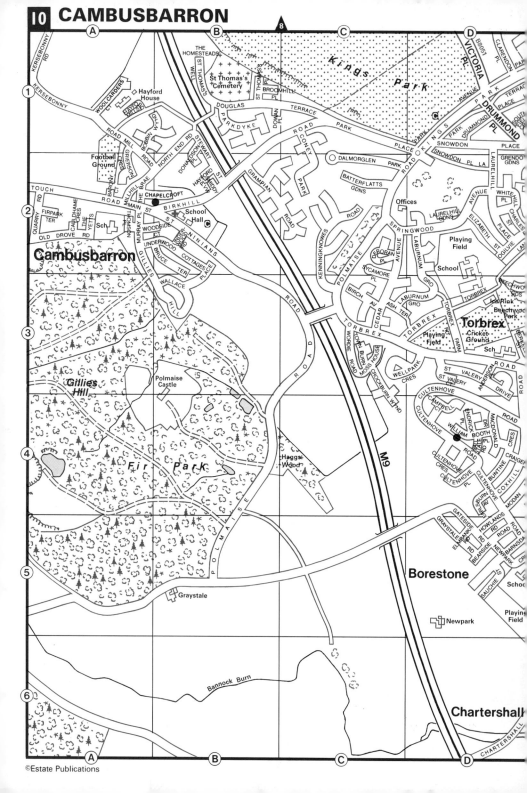

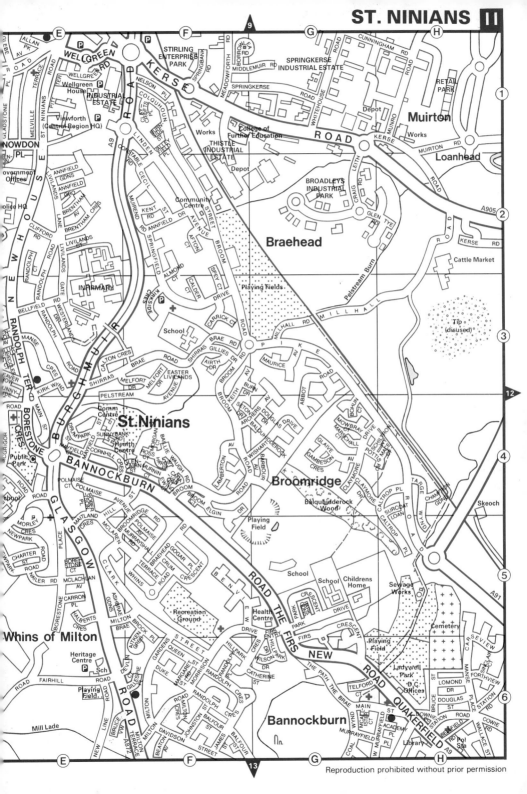

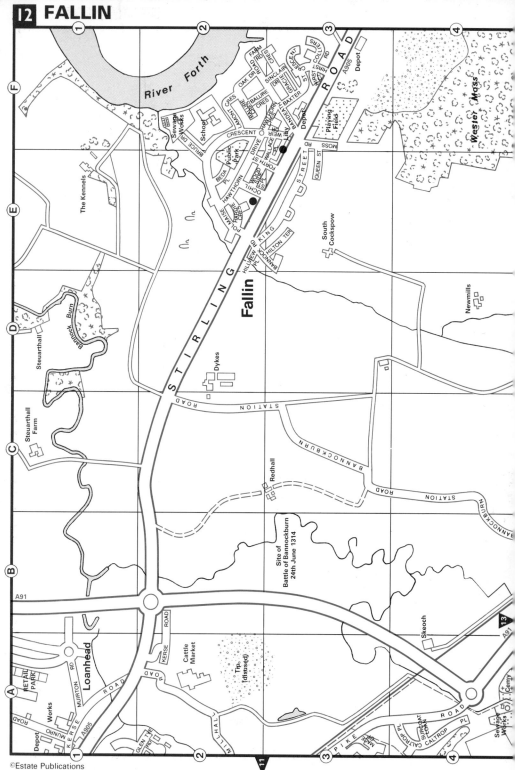

12 FALLIN

River Forth

Wester Moss

Sewage Works

School

BRUCE DR

The Kennels

FARM LOAN RD

OAK DR

SINCLAIR CRES

BALLURE CRES

DRIVE

GRACE ST

BANDEATH ST

FIRST RD

COLLIER RD

A905 Depot

Depot

Playing Field

CRESCENT

RAMONV CRES

Public Park

BEDA PL

HAWTHORN

POLMAISE

FORTH ST

WALLACE ST

WEIR ST

HEATHER

BAXTER

Lilly

MOSS RD

QUEEN ST

STREET

OCHIL

WOOD

STREET

South Cockspow

HILLVIEW RD

KING

BANNOCK PL

HILTON TER

Fallin

STIRLING ROAD

Newmills

Bannock Burn

Steuarthall

Steuarthall Farm

Dykes

Redhall

STATION ROAD

BANNOCKBURN ROAD

STATION ROAD

BANNOCKBURN

Site of Battle of Bannockburn 24th June 1314

Skeoch

A91

KERSE ROAD

MUIRTON RD

Loanhead

RETAIL PARK

Works

Cattle Market

Tip. (disused)

GLEN THE TREE

MILLHAL

KERSE ROAD

A905

Depot

MUNRO ROAD

SPIKE

MAGE ST

SURCOAT LEON

CALTROP PL

CALTROP PL

ROAD

Sewage Works

Cemy

13

A91

©Estate Publications

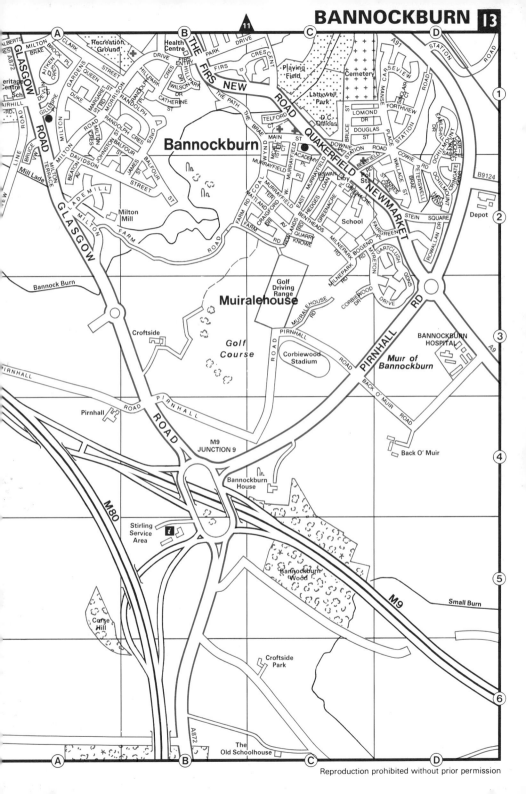

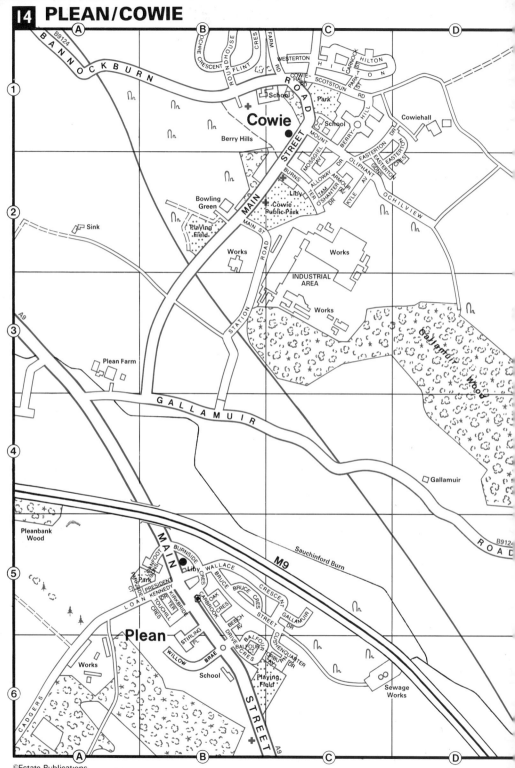

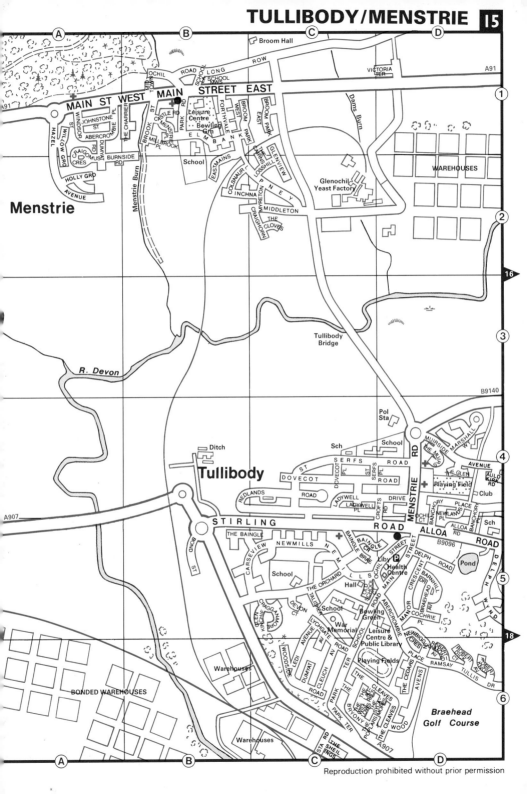

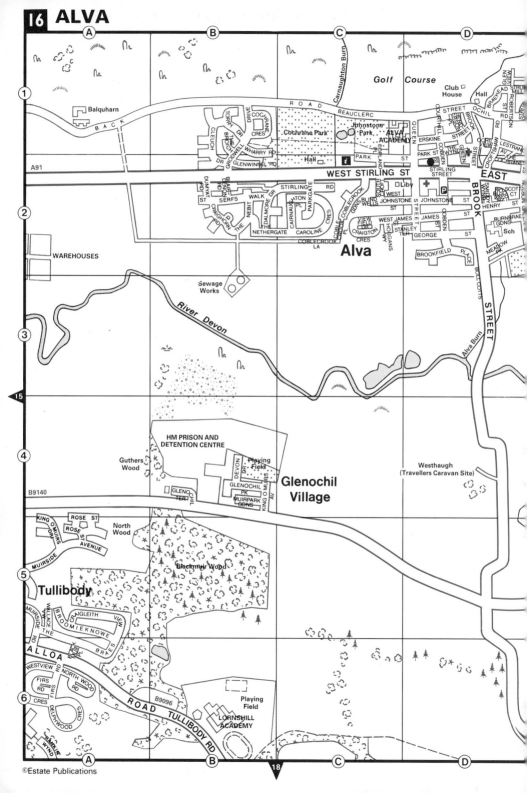

Golf Course

Club House

Hall

Balquharn

A91

WAREHOUSES

Sewage Works

River Devon

15

HM PRISON AND DETENTION CENTRE

Guthers Wood

Playing Field

Glenochil Village

Westhaugh (Travellers Caravan Site)

B9140

North Wood

Blackmeir Wood

Tullibody

ALLOA

Playing Field

LORNSHILL ACADEMY

B9096

TULLIBODY RD

ROAD

Cochrane Park

Johnstone Park

ALVA ACADEMY

WEST STIRLING ST

EAST

Alva

Balquharn

Muirside

King O Muirs

Rose St

Rose Avenue

18

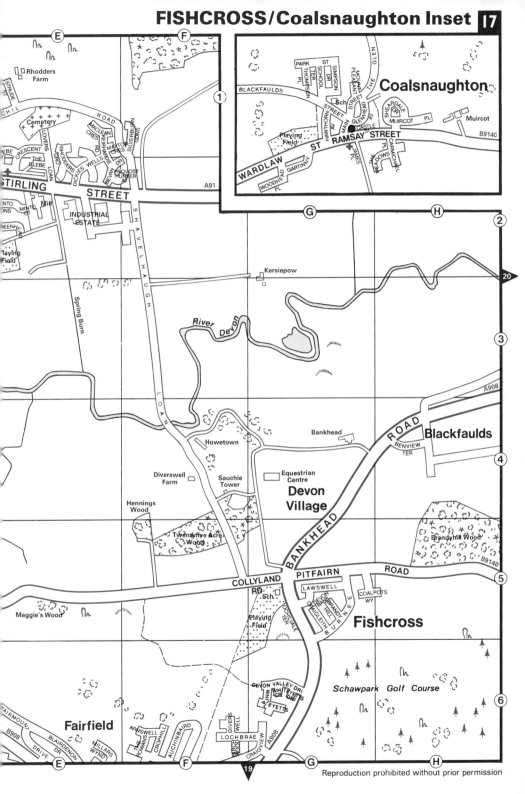

FISHCROSS/Coalsnaughton Inset

Coalsnaughton

BLACKFAULDS

PARK PL
ST TER
THOMSON
DR SCHOOL
SIMPSON
Sch
MOUNT PLEASANT WY
STREET
GLENHEAD
HAWKHILL AV
MAIN STREET
STREET
CASTLE
Playing Field
RAMSAY STREET
WARDLAW ST
JAMES PL
CARMICHAEL PL
WOODHEAD PL
GARTINY
MEADOWS
HEARDALE DR
MUIRCOT PL
Muircot
B9140

A91

E   F   1   G   H   2   20   3

Rhodders Farm

ROAD
Cemetery
MACLEAN CRES
KEIRHARDIE RD
MAXTON CRES
SILVERBURN GDNS
LOVERS GRO
RHODDERS LOAN
DICKIES
WELLS DR
PROVOST HUNTER AV
THE GLEBE
CRESCENT
LOVERS LOAN
STRUDE HILL
GLEBE
MINTO CT
MINTO
Mill

STIRLING   STREET

INDUSTRIAL ESTATE

Playing Field

GREENA...

SHAVELHAUGH

Spring Burn

Kersiepow

River Devon

LOAN

Bankhead

Howetown

Diverswell Farm

Sauchie Tower

Equestrian Centre

Hennings Wood

Twentyfive Acre Wood

ROAD
BENVIEW TER
Blackfaulds
A908

Devon Village

BANKHEAD

Brandyhill Wood

B9140

4   5

COLLYLAND   RD
PITFAIRN   ROAD
LAWSWELL
Sch
COALPOTS WY
DEVON BRANDY HILL
HAUGLEITH B
PITFAIRN
LOCHIVALE TER

Maggie's Wood

Playing Field

Fishcross

Schawpark Golf Course

6

Fairfield

DEVON VALLEY DRI
WHITEYETTS CR
EYETTS
DIVERS WELL
LOCHBRAE
CRAIGVIEW
A908

FAIRMOUNT DRIVE
BLAIRDENON DR
B908
ARNSWELL
CROWANS WYND
CROPHILL
AUCHINBAIRD
MILLARS WYND

E   F   G   H

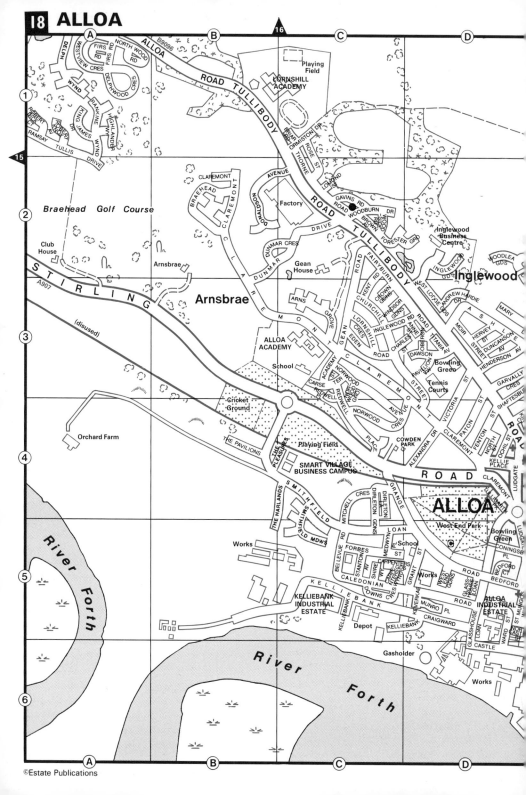

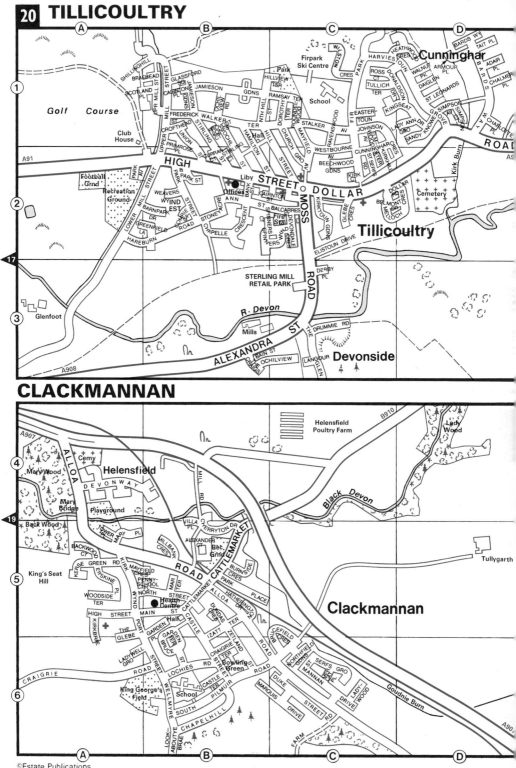

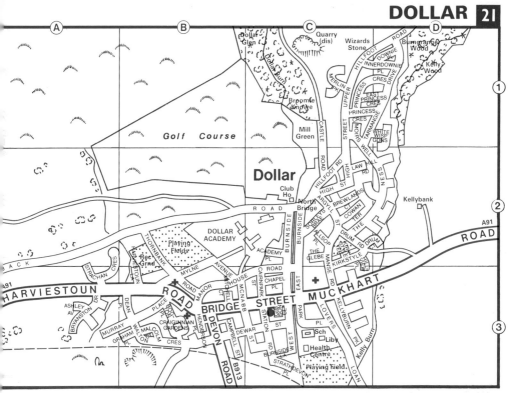

Reproduction prohibited without prior permission

A - Z INDEX TO STREETS
with Postcodes

Bellevue Rd FK10 18 C5
Bellfield Rd, Bannockburn FK7 13 C2
Bellfield Rd, St Ninians FK8 11 E3
Belmont Dri FK13 20 C2
Ben Lomond Dri FK9 8 D1
Bentheads FK7 13 C2
Benview FK7 11 F5
Benview Ter FK10 17 H4
Berkeley St FK7 10 D3
Berryhill FK7 14 C1
Bevan Dri FK12 17 E2
Birch Av FK8 10 C3
Birchwood FK10 19 G1
Birkhill Rd FK7 10 B2
Bishops Gdns FK5 4 C4
Blackfaulds St FK13 Inset 17
Blackmuir Rd FK10 16 A6
Blairdenon Dri FK10 19 E1
Blairdenon Rd FK12 16 B2
Blairforkie Dri FK9 6 C2
Blindwells FK12 16 C2
Bobbin Wynd FK7 10 A1
Boe Ct FK15 5 C5
Bogend Rd FK7 13 C2
Bogside FK15 4 D3
Bogton Pl FK14 21 B3
Bohun Ct FK7 11 G4
Boll Cottages FK12 16 D2
Bond St FK10 18 B5
Borestone Ct FK11 11 E5
Borestone Cres FK7 11 E4
Borestone Pl FK7 11 E5
Borrowlea Rd FK7 11 F1
Borrowmeadow Rd FK7 9 G6
Bowhouse Gdns FK10 19 E6
Bowhouse Rd FK10 19 E6
Braehead Av FK10 15 D5
Braehead Rd FK7 11 F5
Braehead, Alva FK12 16 D1
Braehead, Arnsbrae FK10 18 B2
Braehead, Tillicoultry FK13 20 B1
Braemar Av FK15 5 B5
Braemar Gro FK15 5 B5
Braemar Pk FK15 5 B5
Braeport FK15 4 D4
Braeside FK10 19 F2
Brandy Hill FK10 17 G5
Branshill Pk FK10 19 E2
Branshill Rd FK10 19 E2
Brentham Av FK8 11 E2
Brentham Cres FK8 11 E2
Brewlands St FK14 21 C2
Briar Rd FK10 18 C1
Bridge End FK15 4 C4
Bridge St FK14 21 B3
Bridge Ter*, Shillinghill FK10 19 E5
Bridgehaugh Rd FK9 9 E3
Broad St, Alloa FK10 19 E6
Broad St, Stirling FK8 3 B4
Broadleys Ind Pk FK7 11 G2
Broadleys Rd FK7 9 G6
Brock Pl FK7 11 F5
Brook St, Menstrie FK11 15 B1
Brookfield FK12 16 D2
Broom Ct FK7 11 F4
Broom Pk East FK15 15 C1
Broom Pk West FK11 15 B1
Broom Rd FK7 11 F3
Broomhill Pl FK7 10 B1
Broomieknowe FK10 16 A5
Broomridge Rd FK7 11 F5
Brown Av, Alloa FK10 18 C2
Brown Av, Stirling FK9 8 D1
Bruce Av FK15 4 B4
Bruce Cres FK7 14 B5
Bruce Dri FK7 12 F2
Bruce St, Alloa FK10 19 F4
Bruce St, Bannockburn FK7 13 C1
Bruce St, Clackmannan FK10 20 B6
Bruce St, Plean FK7 14 B5
Bruce St, Stirling FK8 3 C2
Bruce Ter FK10 10 B2
Bruce Vw FK7 11 E6
Brucefield Cres FK10 20 C6
Bryanston Dri FK14 21 A3
Buccleuth Ct FK15 4 C3

Buchan Dri FK15 4 B4
Buchanan Dri FK9 9 F2
Buntine Cres FK7 10 D4
Burgh Mews FK10 19 E5
Burghmuir Rd, St Ninians FK7 11 E4
Burghmuir Rd, Stirling FK8 3 C2
Burleigh Way FK10 19 F5
Burn Dri FK7 11 F3
Burnbrae FK10 19 F3
Burnbrae Gdns FK12 16 D2
Burnee FK10 17 G5
Burns St FK8 9 E3
Burnside Cres, Clackmannan FK10 20 B5
Burnside Cres, Plean FK7 14 B5
Burnside La FK14 21 C3
Burnside Rd FK11 15 A1
Burnside St, Alloa FK10 19 G2
Burnside St, St Ninians FK7 11 F1

Cadgers Loan FK7 14 A1
Cairnaughton Pl FK12 16 C2
Cairnoch Way FK7 13 D1
Cairnpark St FK14 21 C3
Cairnton Pl FK13 20 B1
Cairnton St FK13 20 B3
Calder Ct FK7 11 F3
Caledonian Pl FK15 4 C4
Caledonian Rd FK10 18 C5
Calton Cres FK7 11 E3
Caltrop Pl FK7 11 H4
Cameronian St FK8 3 D6
Campbell Ct FK7 10 D4
Campbell St FK14 21 B3
Canavan Ct FK7 11 F4
Candleriggs FK10 19 E5
Candleriggs Ct*, Candleriggs FK10 19 E5
Carbrook Dri FK7 14 B5
Carlie Av FK9 7 E5
Carmichael Ct FK9 7 E4
Carmichael Pl FK13 Inset 17
Carnock St FK7 14 C1
Caroline Cres FK12 16 C2
Carpenters Gdns FK10 18 C5
Carpenters Wynd FK10 18 C5
Carrick Ct FK7 11 F3
Carron Pl FK7 11 E5
Carsaig Ct FK9 6 D6
Carse of Lecropt Rd FK9 6 A6
Carse Ter FK10 18 C3
Carsebridge Ct FK10 19 F3
Carsebridge Rd FK10 19 F3
Carseview, Bannockburn FK7 13 D1
Carseview, Tullibody FK10 15 B5
Cask Cres FK9 9 F5
Castle Business Pk FK8 8 B3
Castle Ct*, Castle Rd FK11 15 B1
Castle Ct FK8 3 B3
Castle Rd, Dollar FK14 21 C2
Castle Rd, Menstrie FK11 15 B1
Castle Rd, Stirling FK9 9 F2
Castle Rd, Alloa FK10 18 C3
Castle St, Clackmannan FK10 20 B5
Castle St, Coalsnaughton FK13 Inset 17
Castle Ter FK10 20 B6
Castle Wynd FK8 3 B4
Castlevale FK9 8 D1
Castleview Dri FK9 6 D4
Catherine St FK7 13 B1
Cattlemarket FK10 20 B5
Cauldhame Cres FK7 10 A2
Causewayhead Rd FK8 3 C1
Cawder Gdns FK9 6 C4
Cawder Rd FK9 6 C4
Cawdor Cres FK15 4 B4
Cecil St FK7 11 F2
Cedar Av FK8 10 C3
Centenary Wk FK9 6 D5
Chalmers Pl FK13 20 D1
Chalton Ct FK9 7 F4
Chalton St FK9 7 E3
Chamfron Gdns FK7 11 H4

Chapel Pl FK14 21 C3
Chapelcroft FK7 10 A2
Chapelhill FK10 20 B6
Chapelle Cres FK13 20 B2
Charles Av*, Queens Av FK9 7 E4
Charles Rodger Pl FK9 7 E5
Charles St, Alloa FK10 18 C3
Charles St, Dunblane FK15 5 C5
Charlotte Pl FK13 20 D1
Charter St FK7 11 E5
Chartershall Rd FK7 10 D5
Chattan Av FK9 9 E1
Cherryton Dri FK10 20 B5
Chisholm Av, Cornton FK9 9 E2
Chisholm Av, Dunblane FK15 4 D3
Church Gro, Alloa FK10 19 E2
Church Gro, Tillicoultry FK13 20 C1
Church St FK10 19 E5
Churchill Dri FK9 6 D5
Churchill St FK10 19 E5
Clackmannan Rd FK10 19 F4
Claremont Dri FK9 7 F3
Claremont, Alloa FK10 18 D4
Claremont, Arnsbrae FK10 18 B2
Clarendon Pl, Dunblane FK15 5 C5
Clarendon Pl, Stirling FK8 3 B6
Clarendon Rd FK8 3 B5
Clark St FK7 11 E5
Claycrofts Pl FK7 11 F1
Claymore Dri FK7 11 G4
Cleuch Av FK10 15 C6
Cleuch Dri FK12 16 B1
Cleuch Rd FK9 9 F2
Clifford Rd FK8 11 E2
Coal Wynd FK7 13 C2
Coalgate FK10 19 E5
Coalpots Way FK10 17 G5
Cobden St FK12 16 D1
Cobden St FK12 16 D2
Coblecrook Gdns FK12 16 C2
Coblecrook La FK12 16 C2
Cochrane Cres FK12 16 C2
Cochrie Pl FK10 15 D5
Coldstream Av FK15 4 B4
Colliers Ct*, Balcarres St FK13 20 C2
Colliers Rd FK7 12 F3
Collyland Rd FK10 17 F5
Colquhoun St FK7 11 F1
Colsnaur FK11 15 B2
Colville Gdns*, Ludgate FK10 18 D5
Comrie Ct FK13 20 B2
Coney Pk FK7 10 C1
Coneyhill Rd FK9 7 E4
Coningsby Pl FK10 18 D5
Constable Rd FK7 11 F2
Cooperage Quay FK8 9 G5
Cooperage Way FK10 19 G3
Copland Pl FK12 16 D1
Coppermine Pth FK9 7 E3
Corbiewood Dri FK7 13 C3
Corn Exchange Rd FK8 3 C5
Cornhill Cres FK7 11 E4
Cornton Business Pk FK9 9 E2
Cornton Cres FK9 6 D5
Cornton Rd, Bridge of Allan FK9 6 D4
Cornton Rd, Stirling FK9 9 E2
Courthill FK12 16 D1
Cowan Ter FK14 21 C2
Cowane St FK8 3 C2
Cowden Pk FK10 18 C4
Cowie Ct FK7 13 D2
Cowiehall Rd FK7 10 D4
Coxburn Brae FK9 6 D1
Coxhill Rd FK10 20 C1
Cragganmore FK10 15 C6
Craig Ct FK9 7 E5
Craig Cres FK9 9 G2
Craig Leith Rd FK7 11 G2
Craigbank FK10 19 F2

Craigend Rd FK7 10 D4
Craigford Dri FK7 13 C2
Craigforth Cres FK8 8 C4
Craighall St FK8 3 C2
Craighorn FK11 15 C2
Craighorn Rd FK12 16 B2
Craiginnian Gdns FK14 21 B3
Craiglea FK9 9 G2
Craigleith Vw FK10 16 A5
Craigleith FK10 17 G5
Craigomus Cres FK11 15 A1
Craigrie Rd FK10 20 A6
Craigrie Ter FK10 20 B6
Craigton Cres FK12 16 C2
Craigview FK10 19 G1
Craigward FK10 18 D5
Cringate Gdns FK7 13 D2
Crockburn Wynd FK7 10 C3
Crofthead FK13 20 B1
Crofthead Ct FK8 3 B3
Crofthead Rd FK8 3 B3
Crofts Rd FK10 15 D4
Croftshaw Rd FK10 15 D4
Cromlix Cres FK15 4 B4
Crophill FK10 19 F1
Crosbies Ct FK8 3 C6
Crown Gdns FK10 18 C3
Cruachan Av FK9 9 E2
Crum Cres FK7 11 F5
Cultenhove Cres FK7 10 D4
Cultenhove Pl FK7 10 D4
Cultenhove Rd FK7 10 D4
Cunningham Dri FK13 20 C2
Cunningham Rd FK7 11 G1
Curran Ct FK13 20 B2
Cushenquarter Dri FK7 14 C6

Daiglen Ct FK13 20 D1
Dalgleish Ct FK8 3 C4
Dalmore Dri FK12 16 B2
Dalmorglen Pk FK7 10 C2
Dargai Ter FK15 4 C3
Darn Rd, Bridge of Allan FK9 6 C2
Darn Rd, Dunblane FK15 5 D5
Darnley St FK8 3 B4
Davidson St FK7 13 A2
Dawson Av FK10 18 D3
Dean Cres FK8 3 D2
Dean Pl FK14 21 B3
Deerpark FK10 19 H2
Delph Rd FK10 15 C4
Delph Wynd FK10 15 D5
Delphwood Cres FK10 16 A6
Derby Pl FK13 20 C2
Dermoch Dri FK15 4 B4
Deroran Pl FK8 10 C2
Devlin Ct FK7 11 E6
Devon Bank FK10 17 G5
Devon Ct FK10 15 C5
Devon Dri FK10 16 B4
Devon Rd, Alloa FK10 19 F5
Devon Rd, Dollar FK14 21 B3
Devon Valley Dri FK10 19 G1
Devondale Cres FK13 20 C2
Devonway FK10 20 A4
Dewar St FK14 21 B3
Dickies Wells FK12 17 E2
Dirleton Gdns FK10 18 C4
Dirleton La FK10 18 C4
Diverswell FK10 19 G1

Dockburn Ind Est FK15 5 C5
Dollar Rd FK13 20 C2
Donaldson Av FK10 18 B2
Donaldson Dri FK13 20 C1
Donaldson Pl FK7 10 B2
Doo'Cot Brae FK10 18 D3
Dorothy Ter FK13 20 C1
Douglas Dri FK13 20 C1
Douglas Pk FK15 5 B5
Douglas St, Bannockburn FK7 13 C1
Douglas St, Stirling FK8 3 C2
Doune Rd FK15 4 A3
Dovecot Pl FK10 18 D1
Dovecot Rd FK10 15 C4
Dovehill FK10 19 E3
Dowan Pl FK7 10 B1
Downie Pl, Bannockburn FK7 13 C1
Downie Pl, Dollar FK14 21 D1

Downs Cres FK10 18 C5
Drip Rd FK8 3 B1
Drum Ct FK14 21 C2
Drum Rd FK14 21 C2
Drummie Rd FK13 20 C3
Drummond Pl FK8 10 D1
Drummond Pl La FK8 10 D1
Drummond Rise FK15 4 D4
Drumpark St FK7 11 E4
Drysdale St FK10 19 E5
Duff Cres FK8 8 C4
Duke St*, Beauclerc St, Alva FK12 16 D1
Duke St, Clackmannan FK10 20 C6
Duke St, St Ninians FK7 11 F6
Dumbarton Rd FK8 3 C5
Dumyat Av FK10 15 C6
Dumyat Rd, Alva FK12 16 B2
Dumyat Rd, Menstrie FK11 15 A1
Dumyat Rd, Stirling FK9 9 F2
Duncanson Av FK10 18 D3
Dundas Cres FK10 20 B5
Dundas Rd FK9 9 E1
Dunmar Cres FK10 18 B2
Dunmar Dri FK10 18 B2
Dunster Rd FK9 9 F2
Dunvegan Ct FK10 19 F5
Dunvegan Dri FK9 9 F3
Dykedale FK15 4 E4

Earl of Mar Ct FK10 19 E5
Earls Ct FK10 19 E6
Earlsburn Av FK7 10 D4
Earlshill Dri FK7 13 D1
Earn Ct FK10 19 F5
East Burnside FK14 21 C3
East Castle St FK10 19 E6
East Mains FK11 15 B2
East Murrayfield FK7 13 C2
East Princess Cres FK14 21 C1
East Stirling St FK12 16 D2
East Vennel FK10 19 E5
Easter Cornton Rd FK9 9 E1
Easter Livilands FK7 11 F3
Easterton Cres FK7 14 C2
Easterton Dri FK7 14 C2
Easterton Gdns FK7 14 C2
Eastertoun FK13 20 C1
Easton Ct FK8 9 E3
Eccles St FK7 11 E3
Eden Rd FK10 18 C3
Edward Av FK8 9 F4
Edward Pl FK15 5 C5
Edward Rd FK8 3 D2
Edward St FK15 5 C5
Elgin Ct FK7 11 F4
Elistoun Dri FK13 20 C2
Elizabeth St FK8 10 D2
Elm Gro FK10 19 F6
Elm St FK8 8 C4
Elmbank FK11 15 B1
Elmbank Rd FK7 10 D5
Elmwood Av FK13 20 C1
Endrick Pl FK7 10 D4
Engelen Dri FK10 19 E6
Erskine Ct FK8 8 B3
Erskine Pl FK10 20 A5
Erskine St, Alloa FK10 19 E4
Erskine St, Alva FK12 16 D1
Etive Pl FK9 9 E2
Ewing Ct FK7 11 F4

Fairfield FK10 19 E1
Fairgreen Pl FK7 11 E1
Fairhill Rd FK7 11 E6
Fairmount Dri FK10 18 C2
Fairyburn Rd FK10 18 C2
Farm Rd, Bannockburn FK7 13 C2
Farm Rd, Clackmannan FK10 20 C6
Farm Rd, Cowie FK7 14 C1
Farm Rd, Fallin FK7 12 F2
Fenton St FK10 18 D4
Ferguson St FK8 8 D3
Ferndene Ter*, New Rd FK7 13 B1
Ferniebank Brae FK9 6 C2
Ferry Ct FK9 9 G4
Ferry Rd FK9 9 G4
Ferry Orchard FK9 9 G4
Fir Park FK13 20 C1
Firpark Ter FK7 10 A2

Firs Cres FK7 11 G5
Firs Entry FK7 11 G5
Firs Rd FK10 16 A6
Fishermans Wk FK9 8 D2
Fishers Grn FK9 6 D1
Flint Cres FK7 14 B1
Forbes St FK10 18 C5
Forebraes FK10 19 E4
Forester Gro FK10 18 C2
Forglen Cres FK9 7 E5
Forglen Rd FK9 7 E5
Forrest Rd FK8 3 D2
Forth Ct FK8 3 D2
Forth Cres, Alloa FK10 19 F6
Forth Cres, Stirling FK8 3 D3
Forth Park FK9 6 D6
Forth Pl FK8 3 D3
Forth St, Fallin FK7 12 E2
Forth St, Stirling FK8 3 D2
Forthvale FK11 15 B1
Forthview,
  Bannockburn FK7 13 D1
Forthview, Stirling FK8 3 D2
Fountain Rd FK9 6 D4
Fraser Pl FK9 9 E1
Frederick St FK13 20 B1
Friars St FK8 3 C5

Gaberston Av FK10 19 F4
Gallamuir Ct FK7 14 C5
Gallamuir Rd FK7 14 B4
Gambeson Cres FK7 11 G4
Garden Pl FK10 20 B5
Garden Ter FK10 20 B6
Gartclush Gdns FK7 13 D2
Gartinny FK13 Inset 17
Gartmorn Rd FK10 19 G2
Garvally Cres FK10 18 D3
Gateside Rd FK7 10 D5
Gavins Rd FK10 18 C2
Gean Rd FK10 18 C2
George St, Alva FK12 16 D2
George St,
  Dunblane FK15 5 C5
Gibson Clo FK14 21 C3
Gibson Gro FK15 5 E5
Gillespie Pl FK7 11 F6
Gillies Dri FK7 11 F3
Gillies Hill FK7 10 A2
Gladstone Pl FK8 11 E1
Glaive Av FK7 11 G4
Glasgow Rd FK7 11 E4
Glassford Sq FK13 20 B1
Glasshouse Loan FK10 18 D5
Glebe Av FK8 3 B6
Glebe Cres, Alva FK12 17 E1
Glebe Cres, Stirling FK8 3 B6
Glebe Cres,
  Tillicoultry FK13 20 C2
Glebe Pl FK15 4 C4
Glebe Ter FK10 19 E5
Glen Ct FK15 4 E4
Glen Kinchie FK10 15 C5
Glen Rd,
  Bridge of Allan FK9 6 D2
Glen Rd,
  Dunblane FK15 5 D4
Glen Tye Rd FK7 11 G2
Glen View FK12 16 D1
Glenallan Ct FK15 5 C5
Glencairn St FK7 11 F4
Glencoe Rd FK8 3 B2
Glendevon Dri FK8 3 A1
Glenhead Av FK7 Inset 17
Glenochil Pk FK10 16 B4
Glenochil Ter FK10 16 B4
Glenview FK11 15 C2
Glenwinnel Rd FK12 16 B2
Gogar Pl FK7 11 F5
Goosecroft Rd FK8 3 C3
Gordon Cres,
  Bridge of Allan FK9 6 D3
Gordon Cres,
  Stirling FK8 8 C3
Gordon Dri FK10 19 F3
Gowanhill Gdns FK8 3 A1
Gracie Cres FK7 12 F3
Graham Av,
  Dunblane FK15 4 D2
Graham Av,
  Stirling FK9 9 G1
Graham Pl FK14 21 B3
Graham St FK9 7 E4
Grampian Rd FK10 10 B2
Grange Gdns FK9 7 F4
Grange Rd FK10 18 C4

Grant Dri FK15 4 B3
Grant Pl FK9 9 E2
Grant St FK10 18 D5
Graystale Rd FK10 10 D5
Greenacre Ct FK7 13 C2
Greenacre Pl FK7 13 C2
Greenfield La FK13 20 B2
Greenfield St FK10 19 F3
Greenhead FK12 16 D2
Greenside St FK10 19 E5
Greenwood Av FK8 3 A4
Grendon Ct FK8 11 E2
Grendon Gdns FK8 10 D2
Greygoran FK10 19 F1
Grierson Cres FK7 10 A2
Grodwell Dri FK12 16 B2

Haig Av FK8 9 E3
Haining FK15 4 C3
Halberts Cres FK7 11 E5
Haldane Av FK9 7 E5
Hallpark FK10 19 F3
Hamilton Dri FK9 9 F1
Hamilton St FK13 20 B1
Hanover Ct,
  Causewayhead FK9 9 G1
Hanover Ct,
  Dunblane FK15 5 C5
Hardie Cres FK7 12 E2
Hareburn Rd FK13 20 A2
Harris Ct FK10 19 E6
Hart Wynd FK7 13 D2
Harvest St CL9 8 D1
Harvey Wynd FK8 3 D2
Harviestoun Gro FK13 20 C1
Harviestoun La FK7 21 B3
Harviestoun Rd FK14 21 A3
Hatherington Dri FK10 20 B5
Haugh Rd FK9 9 E3
Hawkhill Rd FK10 19 F5
Hawthorn Av FK13 Inset 17
Hawthorn Cres,
  Fallin FK7 12 F3
Hawthorn Cres,
  Stirling FK8 8 D3
Hawthorn Dri FK7 12 E2
Hayford Mills FK7 10 A1
Hayford FK7 10 B2
Hazel Av FK11 15 A1
Hazelbank Gdns FK8 8 D3
Heathwood Cres FK13 20 D1
Hedges Loan FK7 13 C2
Henderson Av FK10 18 D3
Henderson Pl,
  Alva FK12 16 D1
Henderson Pl,
  Dollar FK14 21 B3
Henderson St FK9 6 D3
Henry Milne Wk FK7 7 H5
Henry St FK12 16 D2
Hepburn Ct FK15 4 D2
Hermitage Rd FK9 7 G5
Hervey Rd FK10 18 D3
High St, Alloa FK10 19 E5
High St,
  Clackmannan FK10 20 A5
High St, Dollar FK14 21 C2
High St, Dunblane FK15 4 D4
High St,
  Tillicoultry FK13 20 B2
Highfields FK15 5 B5
Highlander Way FK10 18 A1
Hill Pk FK10 19 E4
Hill Rd FK10 19 E3
Hill St, Alloa FK10 19 E4
Hill St, St Ninians FK7 11 E4
Hill St,
  Tillicoultry FK13 20 B1
Hillcrest Dri FK10 19 F5
Hillfoot Rd FK14 21 C2
Hillfoots Rd FK9 9 G1
Hillpark Cres FK7 13 B1
Hillpark Dri FK7 13 B1
Hillside FK10 19 F1
Hillside Av FK15 5 C5
Hillside Ter FK10 19 E4
Hillview Dri FK9 7 E4
Hillview Pl,
  Dollar FK14 21 C2
Hillview Pl, Fallin FK7 12 E2
Hillview Ter,
  Alloa FK10 19 F5
Hillview Ter,
  Tillicoultry FK13 20 B1
Hilton FK7 14 C1

Hilton Cres FK10 19 G4
Hilton Rd FK10 19 F4
Hilton Ter FK7 12 E3
Hiltonhawk Way FK10 19 F5
Hirst Ct FK7 12 F3
Hirst Cres FK7 12 F3
Hoggans Way FK12 16 C2
Holbourne Pl*,
  Main St East FK11 15 B1
Holly Gro FK10 19 E5
Holme Hill Ct FK15 4 D4
Holton Cotts FK10 19 F2
Holton Ct*,
  Holton Cres FK10 19 F2
Holton Cres FK10 19 F2
Holton Sq FK10 19 F2
Hope St FK8 8 C4
Hopetoun Dri FK9 6 D3
Howlands Rd FK7 10 D5
Hume Ct FK7 7 E5
Hume Cres FK9 6 D5
Huntley Cres FK8 8 C3
Hutton Pk FK10 19 F4

Inchna FK11 15 B2
Inglewood Gdns FK10 10 D2
Inglewood Rd FK10 18 D3
Ingram Dri FK15 4 D2
Innerdownie Pl FK14 21 C1
Inveralian Ct FK9 6 C3
Inverallan Dri FK10 6 C4
Inverallan Rd FK10 6 C4
Irvine Pl FK8 3 B3
Ivanhoe Pl FK8 8 D3
Izatt Ter FK10 20 B5

Jail Wynd FK8 3 B4
James Pl FK13 Inset 17
James St, Alva FK12 16 D2
James St,
  Bannockburn FK7 13 B2
James St, Stirling FK8 3 D2
Jamieson Gdns FK13 20 B1
Jellyholm Rd FK10 19 G3
John Cadwane Row*
  Ben Lomond Ter FK10
John Murray Dri FK9 6 D3
John R Gray Rd FK15 5 C5
John Rushforth Pl FK8 8 D3
Johnson Av FK9 9 F2
Johnson Cres FK13 20 C1
Johnston St FK7 13 A1
Johnstone Ct*,
  West Johnstone St
  FK12 16 C2
Johnstone St,
  Alva FK12 16 D2
Johnstone St,
  Menstrie FK11 15 A1

Katrine Cres FK10 19 G5
Keilarsbrae FK10 19 F2
Keir Av FK8 9 E3
Keir Ct FK9 7 E4
Keir Gdns FK9 6 D4
Keir Hardie Rd FK12 17 E1
Keir La FK15 5 E5
Keir St,
  Bridge of Allan FK9 6 D4
Keir St,
  Dunblane FK15 4 C4
Keirbrae FK10 19 F4
Kellie Ct FK9 7 F3
Kellie Pl FK10 18 D4
Kellie Wynd FK15 4 E2
Kelliebank FK10 18 C5
Kelliebank Ind Est
FK10 18 C5
Kelly Ct FK8 3 B4
Kellyburn Pk FK14 21 C3
Kenilworth Ct FK9 7 F4
Kenilworth Rd FK9 7 E3
Kenningknowes Rd
  FK8 10 C2
Kent Rd, Alloa FK10 18 C3
Kent Rd,
  St Ninians FK7 11 F2
Kerse Green Rd FK10 20 A5
Kerse Rd FK7 11 F1
Kersebonny Rd FK7 10 A1
Keverkae FK10 18 D5
Kilbryde Ct FK15 4 C4
Kilbryde Cres FK15 4 B3
Kilbryde Gro FK15 4 C3
Kilncraigs Ct FK10 19 F5
Kilncraigs Rd FK10 19 F5
King James Dri FK10 18 A1

King o'Muirs Av FK10 16 B4
King o'Muirs Dri FK10 16 A5
King Robert Ct FK9 8 C4
King St, Fallin FK7 12 E2
King St, Stirling FK8 3 C5
Kings Ct FK10 18 D4
Kings Park Rd FK8 3 B6
Kingseat Dri FK13 20 D1
Kingstables La FK8 3 B3
Kingswell Pk FK10 19 F4
Kinnaird Av FK15 4 B4
Kinnoull Av FK15 4 B4
Kippendavie Av FK15 4 E2
Kippendavie La FK15 4 E2
Kippendavie Rd FK15 4 E2
Kirk Ct FK13 20 C2
Kirk St FK15 4 D4
Kirk Wynd,
  Clackmannan FK10 20 A5
Kirk Wynd,
  St Ninians FK7 11 E3
Kirkbrae FK10 20 A5
Kirkbridge Ter FK10 14 B5
Kirkgate FK10 19 E5
Kirkhill Ter FK13 20 C2
Kirkside Cres FK7 11 F3
Kirkstyle FK14 21 C2
Kirkstyle Ter FK14 21 C2
Kirktoun Gdns FK13 20 C2
Kyle Av FK7 14 C2

Laburnum Gro FK8 10 D2
Lademill FK7 13 A2
Lady Ann Gro FK13 20 D1
Ladysneuk Rd FK9 9 G2
Ladywell Dri FK10 15 C4
Ladywell Gro FK10 20 A6
Ladywell Pl FK10 15 C4
Ladywood FK10 20 C6
Laighhill Ct FK15 4 D3
Laighhill Pl FK15 4 D3
Lambert Ter FK10 19 F4
Lamberton Av FK7 11 F4
Lamont Cres FK7 12 F2
Landrick Av FK15 4 E2
Langour FK13 20 C3
Laurelhill Gdns FK8 10 D2
Laurelhill Pl FK8 10 D2
Laurencecroft Rd FK8 3 C1
Law Hill Rd FK14 21 C2
Lawder Pl FK15 4 E2
Lawswell FK10 17 G5
Ledcamerroch Gdns
  FK15 4 D3
Ledi Av FK10 15 C6
Ledi Vw FK9 9 E2
Leewood Pk FK15 5 E5
Leewood Rd FK15 5 E5
Leighton Av FK15 4 F4
Leighton Ct FK15 4 F4
Lennox Av FK7 11 E3
Lestrange Av FK10 16 D1
Leven Ct FK10 19 F6
Lewis Ct FK10 19 E6
Lilybank Ct FK10 19 G2
Linden Av FK7 11 F1
Lindsay Brae FK15 5 B5
Lindsay Dri FK9 9 E1
Lipney FK11 15 C2
Lister Ct FK9 6 D5
Livilands Ct FK8 11 E2
Livilands Gate FK8 11 E2
Livilands La FK8 11 E2
Loanfoot Gdns FK7 14 B5
Lochbrae FK10 19 G1
Lochies Rd FK10 20 B6
Logie La FK9 7 F4
Logie Rd FK9 9 G1
Lomond Ct, Alloa FK10 19 F6
Lomond Ct,
  Stirling FK9 8 C4
Lomond Cres FK9 9 E1
Lomond Dri FK7 13 C1
Lomond Rd FK10 18 C2
Long Row FK11 15 B1
Lookaboutye Brae
  FK10 20 B6
Lornshill Cres FK10 18 C4
Losshill FK11 15 C2
Lothian Cres FK9 9 F1
Lovers Loan,
  Alva FK12 17 E1
Lovers Loan,
  Dollar FK14 21 C3
Lovers Walk FK10 3 C1
Lower Bridge St FK8 3 C1
Lower Castlehill FK8 3 B3

Lower Mill St FK13 20 A2
Ludgate FK10 18 D4
Lychgate Rd FK10 15 C6
Lyon Cres FK9 6 D4

McAlley Ct FK9 6 D4
McAllister Ct FK7 13 C1
Macdonald Dri FK7 10 D5
Mace Ct FK7 11 H4
McGrigor Rd FK7 11 E4
McKinlay Cres FK10 19 F4
McLachlan Av FK7 11 E5
McLaren Ter FK7 11 E5
Maclean Cres FK12 17 E1
McNabb St FK14 21 B3
McPherson Dri FK8 8 D3
Main St East FK11 15 B1
Main St West FK11 15 A1
Main St,
  Bannockburn FK7 13 C1
Main St,
  Cambusbarron FK7 10 A2
Main St,
  Clackmannan FK10 20 B5
Main St,
  Coalsnaughton
  FK13 Inset 17
Main St, Cowie FK7 14 B2
Main St,
  New Sauchie FK10 19 F2
Main St, Plean FK7 14 B5
Main St,
  St Ninians FK7 11 E4
Main St,
  Tullibody FK10 15 D5
Maitland Av FK7 13 C2
Maitland Cres FK7 11 E5
Malcolm Ct FK14 21 B3
Mannan Dri FK10 20 C6
Manor Cres FK10 15 D5
Manor House Rd FK14 21 B3
Manse Cres FK7 11 E3
Manse Pl FK7 13 D1
Manse Rd FK14 21 C2
Manse Ter*,
  Port St FK10 20 B5
Mansfield St FK10 19 G2
Maple Ct FK10 19 E5
Mar Pl, Alloa FK10 19 E4
Mar Pl,
  New Sauchie FK10 19 F2
Mar Pl, Stirling FK8 3 B3
Mar St FK10 19 E5
Mar Ter FK10 20 B5
Marchside Ct*,
  Holton Cres FK10 19 F2
Maree Ct FK10 19 F5
Margaret Rd FK7 11 F6
Marlborough Dri FK9 9 F2
Marquis Dri FK10 20 C6
Marschall Ct FK7 11 G4
Marshall Way FK10 15 D4
Marshill FK10 19 E5
Mary Pl FK10 20 A5
Mary Stevenson Dri
  FK10 18 D3
Maurice Av FK7 11 G3
Maxton Cres FK12 17 E1
Maxwell Pl FK8 3 C4
Mayfield Av FK13 20 C1
Mayfield Ct FK7 11 E4
Mayfield Cres FK10 20 A5
Mayfield FK7 11 E4
Mayne Av FK9 7 E4
Meadow Grn FK10 19 E2
Meadow Pk FK12 16 D2
Meadow Pl FK8 9 F4
Meadowforth Rd FK7 11 F1
Meadowland Rd FK9 7 E4
Medwyn Pl FK10 18 C5
Melfort Rd FK7 11 F3
Melloch Cres FK13 20 C2
Melville Pl FK8 7 E4
Melville Ter FK8 3 C6
Menstrie Pl FK11 15 B1
Menstrie Rd FK10 15 D4
Menteith Ct FK10 19 F5
Menteith Rd FK9 9 E2
Menteith Vw FK15 4 E3
Menzies Ct FK8 8 D3
Mercat Pl FK10 20 C6
Mercat Wynd FK10 19 E5
Merlin Pk FK14 21 C1
Middlemuir Rd FK7 11 F1
Middleton FK11 15 C2
Midtown FK11 15 C2